ats are *better* than Dogs

Cats are *better* than Dogs

JEAN NORMAN

illustrations by Eric Löbbecke

HarperCollins*Publishers*

HarperCollins*Publishers*

First published in Australia in 1996
by HarperCollins*Publishers* Pty Limited
ACN 009 913 517
A member of the HarperCollins*Publishers* (Australia) Pty Limited Group

HarperCollins*Publishers*
25 Ryde Road, Pymble, Sydney NSW 2073, Australia
31 View Road, Glenfield, Auckland 10, New Zealand
77–85 Fulham Palace Road, London W6 8JB, United Kingdom
Hazelton Lanes, 55 Avenue Road, Suite 2900, Toronto, Ontario M5R 3L2
and 1995 Markham Road, Scarborough, Ontario M1B 5M8 Canada
10 East 53rd Street, New York NY 10032, USA

National Library of Australia Cataloguing-in-Publication data:

Norman Jean, 1965
Cats are *better* than dogs.
ISBN 0 7322 5713 1.
I. Cats – Humor. 2. Dogs – Humor. I. Title
636.800207

Printed in Australia by Griffin Paperbacks
9 8 7 6 5 4 3 2 1   96 97 98 99

For Jack and Mark

Cats are animal companions . . . Dogs are pets.

I

Models parade along a runway or 'catwalk' – 'dogwalk' just doesn't have

the same ring to it . . .

Catsuits are sexy, fetishistic fashionwear – does Versace do a Dogsuit?

'She moved with languid, feline grace'. . .

Try substituting 'feline' with 'canine'.

3

Batman would never have fallen in love with Dogwoman.

Al Stewart's classic hit, Year of the Cat, was about an alluring,

spell-binding femme fatale . . .

Did the songwriter ever consider calling it Year of the Dog?

5

Cats always land on their feet – Dogs fall over their feet.

A Cat can out-stare anyone it feels like out-staring . . .

Dogs always blink first.

7

Given the choice, Cats prefer to recline upon silk, rather than polyester . . .

Dogs just cannot tell the difference.

Cats look cute relaxing in
designer shop windows . . .
Dogs need not apply –
they'd destroy the display
or dribble down the plate
glass windows.

9

Cats, all cats, are naturally gorgeous . . .

For their pets to look even vaguely decorative, Dog People

make dogs endure hours of clipping, shaving and heck knows

what else at Dog Beauty Parlours.

The Cat motto is 'When in doubt – Wash' and they do so often and

daintily. Dog People have to bath dogs to avoid vile consequences.

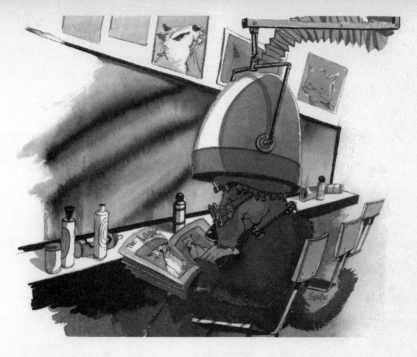

II

Cat noses are cool, cute and at most moist – Dog noses are cold, clammy,

usually dripping and you never know where they have been . . .

Cats practise aromatherapy by luxuriating in sweet-scented catnip . . .

Dogs prefer rolling in dung or pre-loved meat dinners.

13

Nobody ever made a fool of themselves slipping on cat-poo in the street.

Cats, like most humans, do not consider it appropriate

to defecate in public . . .

Dogs see it as not only okay — but de rigeur.

15

If Cats are unavoidably caught in the rain they merely become moist

and fragrant – albeit enraged . . .

Dogs don't mind the rain but they should –

for the wet Dog smells like a huge, sweaty sock.

Cats are aristocrats – Dogs are the 'help'. Dogs will lick up anything that's been dropped on the floor . . .

Cat People own mops and do not consider the canine skill of replacing gunk with dog drool a domestic asset.

18

A Cat-burglar is an especially cunning thief . . .

A Dog-burglar would crap on the museum floor, accidentally eat the

diamonds and then throw them back up on someone's front porch later.

21

To say someone has 'Dogbreath' is considered an official insult.

Catbreath? How many Cats do you know with halitosis?

A Catnap is an elegant siesta . . .

A Dognap would no doubt involve drunkenly passing

out in a gutter someplace.

23

Dogs pester and whine for attention . . .

only after telepathy has failed will Cats emit a melodious and polite meow.

Cats purr to express pleasure. Dogs have uncontrollable

quivering of their haunches and often, spontaneous erections

– which Dog People seem to think cute.

25

Cats pick appropriate, same species partners for discreet fun times . . .

Unlike Dogs, they don't attempt to mount human legs

at the slightest opportunity.

Cats rarely display their, er, 'personal' life in public. Dogs seem to

actually prefer an audience.

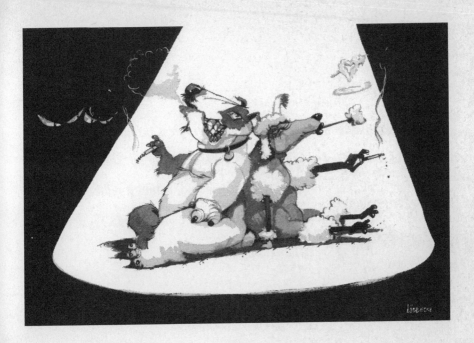

27

When Cats meet each other they progress through a series of complex social manoeuvres – Dogs scuttle up, sniff round for a whiff of one another's bottoms and, within a millisecond, opt for mating or death to the other Dog.

29

Cat people don't stand in the street simpering

'He's really friendly – just don't touch him whatever you do!'

Cats may deign to rub up against the postman's leg . . .

Dogs try to bite the postman's leg.

33

Cats are pacifist creatures – their catfights tend to occur over philosophical differences of opinion. Dogs go to war and get jobs chasing foxes or as riot dogs at the drop of a hat . . .
And, let's face it, Dog People are secretly gleeful when Fido gets into a scrap while they're out walking the thing – you just have to look at their faces.

35

Dog People choose a pet that hurls itself upon the owner

in a panting heap, paws frantically at zips/buttons and shoves

its snout into lewd regions without invitation . . .

Cat People have no need to use animals as fill-in suitors.

The Dog is supposed to be 'Man's Best Friend' – it says a lot about Dog People that they have to feed and house an animal just to get a best friend . . . The Cat – unlike the Dog – is discriminatingly affectionate . . . The Cat is Cat's Best Friend.

Dogs get marched off to obedience school . . .

Cats put their human attendants through an obedience programme.

40

41

When its human companion is away, a Cat merely requires food, water and a catflap. To avoid their incipient nervous breakdown at being left alone, Dogs have to stay at a kennel.

A Dog never knows when it is going to the vet – the Cat has

disappeared days beforehand . . .

Even if it hasn't vanished, The Cat can glean all it needs

to know from the tone in your voice when you call . . .

45

Dogs get lost – Cats merely move house if you don't understand them.

If a Cat is abandoned, it usually has a second-stringer up the road

waiting to audition for the role of Cat companion . . .

If a Dog is dumped it could cover dozens of kilometres chasing those who

have done it wrong so it can slavishly lick them.

47

Cats curl up beside slippers – Dogs bury, drool all over
or devour slippers.

Cats sometimes 'texturise' furniture with their claws
– Dogs rip it to shreds.

A person 'going to the dogs' is someone on the verge of abject failure . . .

such a person is said to have a 'hangdog' expression . . .

Not surprisingly, a satisfied person is described as 'the cat

that got the cream'.

A *black* Cat *can be a witch's trusty helper* — *a black* Dog *would knock over the steaming cauldron with its tail and gobble up the eye of newt.*

53

Dogs have 'A dog's life' . . .

Cats have karmically earned themselves nine lives.

Dogs are easily bored . . .
Cats, in non-active moments,
contemplate the nature of
reality or practise past-life
regression, advanced
meditation techniques
and astral travel.

Dogs howl at the moon . . .

Cats conduct ancient and elaborate Full and New Moon rituals.

Contrary to received wisdom, curiosity did not kill the Cat – the Cat

merely moved onto an even higher astral plane . . .

Curiosity lands Dogs in the pound.

Cats don't get led around on leashes by anyone . . .

Dogs have Mistresses and Masters . . .

Cats are Mistresses or Masters of their own Destiny.

If a Dog Person takes a lover, the Dog will become jealous

or try and lie between the couple in bed . . .

Once introduced, the Cat will simply assume its company

is not required for that evening.

61

Dogs are stupid – Cats are intelligent. Have you ever seen . . .

A Cat chasing a car just so it can bite the hubcap?

. . . or a circus Cat in a party hat riding a tricycle round and round just because a leotarded woman with bad hair tells it to?

. . . or a Cat digging up the backyard for two and a half days to rescue

a buried stick?

Dog people seem to think a Dog is practically eligible for MENSA

if it manages to pick up a stick in its mouth, bring it back,

go and get it again . . .

Cats choose not to engage in such moronic behaviour.

Cats are what we all want to be — freelance creative geniuses . . .

They know how soul-destroying the daily grind can be . . .

A sheep-cat would refuse to herd sheep or compete in sheep-cat trials as it would want the sheep to learn self-expression.

69

Cats are civil libertarians at heart . . .

A drug-cat would only bother sniffing out people smuggling

sardines or catnip . . .

A guard-cat would defend its owner but not property . . .

Cats know you can't take it with you.

Dog people are just not 'us' . . .

How could Cat People not look down upon people who think

Fido farting at the dinner party or rubbing his 'thing' up against

Gran's leg are moments of tender hilarity signifying major

developmental milestones for their pet?

73

Even the coolest dog of all, Snoopy, has such a rich inner life
he is obviously a cat in drag.